CAISTER

CW00669621

BEACH BOATS AND E

BEACH COMPANIES

Towards the latter part of the 18th century fishermen and beachmen all along the East Anglian coastline began to group themselves into organised 'companies' for the purpose of salvage and rescue at sea. These groups became known as beach companies and during the 19th century the coastline between Aldeburgh and Cromer supported at least 26 separate groups. Most coastal communities, including the small fishing village of Caister, had a beach company and Great Yarmouth, at that period a major fishing port, had seven separate such groups, a situation that caused much rivalry and competition when the financial rewards of a salvage mission were at stake.

To understand the origins and formation of these groups of men it is necessary to look back at the difficult conditions that often prevailed for the seafaring folk in the East Anglian coastal waters in the days before radio communication and navigational aids that today are taken for granted. All coastal trade was conducted by sailing vessels, many of which were unseaworthy and carried inexperienced crews. The hazards of the sand-banks off this part of the coast, when combined with poor navigation and winter storms, produced a situation many boats could not cope with. The scale of shipwreck and loss of life can be judged from the following report.

1789 Nov. 1st - 40 vessels ashore between Yarmouth and Southwold.
80 fishing boats wrecked and 120 bodies washed ashore between Yarmouth and Cromer.
1807 Nov. 14th - 144 dead bodies washed ashore in this vicinity after a heavy gale.
1810 Nov. 2nd - Beach from Yarmouth to Wells covered with wrecks and dead bodies after a heavy gale.
1836 Feb. 27th - Great storm. 23 vessels stranded on Yarmouth beach.

These losses must of course be seen in relation to the number of vessels at sea during the period. The Norwich Mercury reported in 1838 that,

A view along the dunes at Caister by C.J. Staniland, probably about 1880. The look-out and beach company shed are on the left.

following a gale, between two and three thousand ships at anchor could be seen from the Yarmouth jetty. When the weather improved several days later and the ships were under sail again, more than three thousand sailed through the Yarmouth Roads, taking five hours.

The men who formed the beach companies were, by necessity, a hardy race, living at a time when most men had to look after themselves and their own interests. Sometimes their claims for services rendered resulted in others not looking on them too favourably. James Haylett, a veteran Caister beachman, when asked during the hearing of a salvage case if it was true that beachmen lived on the misfortunes of others replied "No, on their mistakes." Each man owned a share in his company, giving him the right to a 'dole' from the money received for salvage work, which at times could be a considerable sum. A strict set of rules and regulations governed the company and prevented arguments. Those applying to the Caister company will be looked at in more detail in later pages.

Salvage and rescue dominated the autumn and winter months and during the remainder of the year the various companies would find work in a variety of ways including ferrying fish from boats in the Roads to the beach, ferrying ships stores and pilots, landing passengers and anchor 'swiping', a term used to describe the system of sweeping the sea bed for discarded anchors which could be refurbished and sold at a handsome profit. Each company had a headquarters, usually built on the beach, with a lookout tower where in winter months a continual watch would be kept during bad weather for vessels in distress.

As lifeboats were introduced along the coastline, the first being at Lowestoft in 1801, the beach companies were put in charge and provided the crews. In 1824 the Royal National Institution for the Preserving of Life from Shipwreck was formed and thirty years later the Royal National Lifeboat Institution came into being and by 1858 had accepted overall responsibility for the Norfolk lifeboats and their stations. The beach companies still retained their separate identities and crewed the lifeboats.

In September 1852 Charles Dickens, on a visit to Yarmouth, witnessed a beach rescue by a local company. A ship's boat, with a crew of three, was overturned by the breakers while trying to land at the jetty. Beachmen were soon at hand and after roping themselves together, five waded into the rough seas to rescue the men. In his book 'Household Words' published the following year Dickens wrote about this resecue, finishing his article "Feats like these are continually performed by the Yarmouth beachmen, without their seeming to think that they have done anything extraordinary."

Later in the 19th century coastal shipping became safer following the Merchant Shipping Acts, steam replaced sail and improved navigation and communications resulted in fewer shipwrecks. The decline of the beach companies had begun and by 1907 only one company, the Standard, was operating from Yarmouth beach. After a century of work along the East Anglian coastline they had been made redundant by the industry they had so faithfully served and the beachmen were left to man the lifeboats, work they

A drawing by C.J. Staniland of Caister Gap. In the foreground is the yawl 'Red Jacket' and in the background the beach company look-out.

undertook unhesitatingly but for which they received little financial reward. In 1870 Nall, the Yarmouth historian, wrote " ... of late years the competition of steam tugs has greatly interfered with the gains of the beachmen. They sally out of the haven and intercept the beachmen's prizes and also render ships' masters more independent of their aid. The beachmen complain bitterly that when a valuable cargo is the prize, the steamers get before them, but is case of wreck and where human lives only are at stake, they are suffered to risk theirs in the rescue unopposed."

One company, the Caister beach company, survived the decline longer than most, remaining until a motor lifeboat was brought to the village in 1941. The 1970s saw the local beachmen reform into a group that today has many similarities with the beach company that has been part of the village history for almost two hundred years.

THE CAISTER COMPANY

The earliest indications of a Caister beach company come from records of the 1790s when a small group of men, probably 10 to 15 in number, were involved in salvage work. A few names have survived from these early records and among the founder members of the company were

Members of the Caister beach company on the steps of the shed, circa 1880.

John Bickers, Henry Key, William Hunn, George Horth, Thomas London and John Smith. The open boats used for salvage work along this coastline were known as yawls, a name said to be derived from the Scandinavian word jolle, and in 1803 the Caister men were using a yawl called 'Assistance' for their work. In 1816 the yawl 'Prince Blucher' was built for them at Yarmouth and another in 1829. This latter boat, called 'Storm', was a three masted, lugger rigged boat built at the Yarmouth yard of Francis Holmes and Co., the master being Edward Davey and the ownership divided into 64 shares (a common method of boat ownership) held by 28 men from Caister, one man from Scratby and one man from Ormesby.

Other yawls of the period were 'Edward' and 'Industry' whilst amongst the smaller boats, gigs and cobbles were called 'Star' and 'Persivity'.

The population of the village in 1801 was less than 500 but from about 1815 this was steadily increased by families migrating from villages to the north, especially Winterton and California. The reason for this migration was to enable the menfolk to be closer to the Yarmouth fishing industry, which was expanding at that time, but a spin off from this was an increase in experienced men to assist the local beachmen. This influx of experience put the beach company on a firm foundation and by 1836 the company consisted of 30 men, rising to 40 by 1845.

Family names that have become associated with the beachmen and lifeboats over the years, names such as Brown, Haylett, George and many others came to the village during this period. Before 1845 there were only a few buildings, such as the Manor House, Old Mill Farm and the corn mill east of Victoria Street (known then as Horn Street) and it was for this increasing population of seafaring folk that the houses and cottages forming Clay Road and the eastern end of Beach Road were built, either facing or close to the sand dunes and the sea. With so many people having a common surname, nicknames abounded, like the Brown brothers "Whampo", "Noll", "Nat" and "Virgin" or later another Brown family "Hilton", "Shar" and "Puddins".

Account books from the year 1841, although not showing the amount of salvage money doled out to members of the company, give interesting facts about the company workings. Miscellaneous expenses were carefully recorded including the purchase of a one pound candle for the lantern for 6d, 100 nails for 10d and 1d for ink to write up the account book. Milk for the company cat did not escape the expense sheet while on the income side they charged 2/7d (13p) for a yawl to make a trip to the Newarp lightship and £1/11/5d (£1.57p) for the 'William' to go to the aid of a schooner on the beach. For the 'Star' and 'William' to go to the aid of a brig on the beach the company received £12/4/6d (£12.22p).

In September 1841 a subscription was raised to try and establish a lifeboat on the Caister beach and in January 1845 the Bacton lifeboat was

Beach company boats, circa 1915. Behind the lifeboat 'Nancy Lucy' are the yawl 'Eclat' and the gig 'Ubique'; in front is the 'Wasp'.

transferred to Caister by the Norfolk Shipwreck Association. This first lifeboat for the village arrived complete with gear and the materials to build a shed on the beach. The Lord of the Manor, Thomas Clowes, gave his permission for the shed to be erected and described the boat as " ... a small one, about two thirds the size of the Yarmouth boat, out of repair and leaky. In landing her at Caister she was damaged and full of water."

The beachmen were not satisfied with the condition of this boat and in February refused to take it to sea. The Norfolk Shipwreck Association then decided to take steps to establish an efficient station at Caister and to obtain a boat similar to the Yarmouth lifeboat, "of oak, copper fastened, at a cost of not more that £150." This boat was built by Branford of Yarmouth, of the Norfolk and Suffolk type and stationed at Caister from 1846 until 1865.

Lifeboats were maintained by the Norfolk Shipwreck Association and crewed by the beach companies on the condition they were used for lifesaving only. The beachmen had to use their yawls and gigs to respond to salvage calls, but in many cases both the lifeboat and a yawl would put to sea for a mission as will be seen later. In September 1846 the Rector of Caister, Rev. G. Steward, gave the company 38 cork lifesavers "in testimony of his sincere regard for their temporal and spiritual welfare". These were to be kept in the company stores as their joint property and for their use while employed as beachmen of the Caister company.

A new store and lookout was built on the beach in 1846 near the end of

Beach Road, the lookout being raised sixty feet above the beach at the top of a ship's mast the company purchased from Yarmouth for £3/10s (£3.50p). This building, built with permission of the Lord of the Manor, was to remain on the beach for almost the next hundred years, although repaired and altered many times.

Three members of the company, two of them founder members James Church and Robert Howes, were drowned in June 1847 when a company yawl, returning from taking an anchor into Yarmouth harbour, capsized. Only one member of the crew, John Haylett, escaped after managing to swim ashore, probably as he was the youngest of a rather elderly crew.

A poster advertising the sale of a share the beach company.

CAISTER,
Next Gt. Yarmouth.

R. HICKLING

Has received instructions from Mr. SAMUEL SMITH, to sell by auction,

On FRIDAY, 27th of December, 1861,
AT THE LORD NELSON INN, CAISTER,
At SEVEN o'clock in the Evening,

ONE WHOLE FORTIETH SHARE
OF THE
CAISTER SALVAGE

BOATS

Belonging to the Caister Company of Beachmen, with all accumulations of Stock applicable thereto.

The Auctioneer particularly invites the attention of Beachmen and others to the above Sale.

For further particulars apply to Mr. JOHN CLOWES, Solicitor, Regent Street; or to the Auctioneer, Priory Plain, Great Yarmouth.

DENEW, Printer, 72, Hall Plain, Yarmouth.

The beachmen in their red caps for lifeboat day, 1926. The 'James Leath' was the last lifeboat on the Caister No. 1 station.

RULES AND REGULATIONS

As previously stated all beach companies worked to a strict set of rules and the earliest known referring to the Caister company are dated 1848. The company at this time was composed of 40 men and its purpose was "for saving property and rendering assistance to vessels or ships aground, stranded or wrecked on the sands or beach, or in any kind of difficulty, distress or disaster at sea."

The regulations were amended many times over the years but the basic rules on which the company had been founded remained the same, namely that every man who touched a boat belonging to the company as it was being launched to go to a vessel was entitled to an equal share in the earnings of that mission. The money was shared out in accordance with several sets of circumstances that might be encountered; for example when any boat, being the first to reach a vessel and put a man on board belonging to the company, every man belonging to the boat would get a full share. If a second company boat was employed the crew of that boat would be entitled to a seven-eighths share and the crew of a third boat would get a three-quarter share. If the lifeboat was used by the company the crew were entitled to a share in any money received for saving lives.

Men who had been on watch all night in bad weather were entitled to a share of any money earnt up to 1p.m. the next day but any company member absent from the beach, either when the boat was launched or coming ashore, would forfeit his share unless ill or away on company business.

Any member injured undertaking company work was given his share during the period of disability. If medical assistance was required the company would pay. If any man was drowned or fatally injured during company work then his widow would, for a period of twelve months, receive a full share of all earnings and after that period she could nominate someone to work her late husband's share, provided that the company approved the person nominated.

In 1862 an additional rule was made to cover sickness benefit. Any member who fell sick "which sickness is not brought on by his own misconduct" would receive half a share of all that was earnt by the company boats.

LIFEBOATS

The Royal National Lifeboat Insitution took over from the Norfolk Shipwreck Association in 1857 and assumed responsibility for all lifeboats, including the Caister boat. The following year the company acquired a new

The Caister lifeboats 'Nancy Lucy' (left) and 'Covent Garden'. They were both of the Norfolk and Suffolk class, the former being 35ft. and the latter 40ft.

yawl called 'Glance' and gig 'Kitty', the 'Wasp' having been sold for £3-15-0 (£3.75).

In July an agreement was made with Charles Garwood to hire the new gig 'Kitty' to row in the Yarmouth regatta, but there is no record of his achievements. The Yarmouth North Roads Regatta was one of many similar events held along the east coast where beachmen would compete against each other in the yawl and gig races. The competition was fierce and the racing was a serious business for the companies, giving them a chance to test their speed and seamanship against their rivals. The yawl 'Glance' was entered in the regatta by the Caister company for many years.

Membership of the company was strictly limited to 40 shareholders, some shares being handed down from father to son, others sold by auction when the owner retired or left the village. If the new owner of such a share was not acceptable to the company the share had to be sold again. An auction was held at the Lord Nelson public house, Beach Road, on 27th December 1861 to sell the share of Samuel Smith who was going to leave the village and emigrate to America. This was at the period when beach company work was at its height and shares much sought after, a fact reflected in the high price of £84 paid for this one-fortieth share at the auction.

Another yawl, 'Red Jacket', was bought in 1863 to replace some of the older boats and this time it seems that the company invested in a second hand boat as new sails were bought for £28-7-6d (£28.37p). At this time half a ton of coal cost the company 11/3d (57p) and to hire a donkey cart to Yarmouth three times came to 2/4d (12p).

The lookout shed was rebuilt in 1864 and a contemporary account describes the building as follows.

"The shed is in the upper storey a watch-house and beachmen's parliament house where the affairs of the nation (of Caister beachmen) are discussed, accounts settled and business transacted; following up the parallel by even (like other legislators) taking long and comfortable snoozes on the benches which run round the building. One side contains a bay window from which through sliding shutters a view can be obtained north, east or south and where some beachman is always on watch. Two men are on watch every night and all night, taken by rotation from the company;the list hanging up in the shed.Under the shed is a carpenter's shop where the renowned James Vincent manufactures oars, masts, etc. for the company and even condescends to goodwives washing tubs and other domestic appliances."

In 1865 a new lifeboat, a gift of the Birmingham Lifeboat Fund, arrived at Caister. This was a 42 foot boat of the Norfolk and Suffolk design with 14 oars, built by Blake and Mills of Yarmouth at a cost of £238. It was named the 'James Pearce Birmingham No. 2' and was to save 484 lives during its 18 year service at Caister, a record not exceeded by any other lifeboat to come to the station.

Two years later a second lifeboat was stationed at the village, 'The Boys', purchased with a donation from the Routledge Magazine for Boys. This was a smaller boat, 32 feet with 12 oars, built by Beeching of Yarmouth for £152. The company now had two lifeboats to crew as well as their yawls and gigs. In 1875, following a donation to the R.N.L.I. by Lady Bourchier of Hampton Court Palace 'The Boys' was renamed 'Godsend' and three years later the 'James Pearce' was renamed 'Covent Garden', the first of three boats to carry that name, after donations from the Covent Garden Lifeboat Fund.

There were many instances where the company used the lifeboats as well as their yawls for a rescue operation.

"January 17th 1879 - at 6.00 p.m. large flares seen in the direction of the Barber, wind being easterly, launched yawl and rowed to the sands, the small lifeboat ('Godsend') following in case the yawl could not get alongside. Found Brig on the sand, boarded her and agreed with captain to get his vessel off ..."

It is contemporary accounts such as this, extracted from the official R.N.L.I. returns of service, that convey the most accurate picture of some of the work of the beachmen from this period. In some cases the effort and hard work put into launching the boat and rowing or sailing to a vessel, often through hazardous conditions, was not appreciated as an entry for February 28th 1881 shows.

"...Schooner seen coming through Cockle with signal flying from main peak, as the weather was squally, with heavy snow squalls, concluded he was in distress. Launched the No. 2 boat ('Godsend') and proceeded to the vessel, found he had hoisted this signal with the hope of getting a tug quicker, were laughed at by the master and well abused with strong language. Returned to station."

The introduction of steam tugs enabled lifeboats to reach their destination with greater speed, the tug being employed to tow the lifeboat to within a short distance of the vessel in distress and in some cases a combination of yawl, lifeboat and tug was used as this entry of August 1882 illustrates.

"...Schooner on Cross Sand ... master employed beachmen to try and get her off. Sent steam tug for No. 1 lifeboat. Wind died down and yawl got vessel off ... lifeboat rendered no service except standing by in case as there were 21 men in yawl when she left vessel."

Later the same year the lifeboat was launched in reply to flares seen in the direction of the Middle Cross Sand and with the help of a steamship that

The lifeboat 'Covent Garden'. This vessel was on station from 1899 to 1919, being the third to carry the name.

was in the area at the time effected a rescue of eight men. It would seem that no one except the Caister watch saw the distress signals and the company was not slow to bring to the notice of the R.N.L.I. the efficiency of their station by ending their report "...the Caister men hope the committee will favourably consider the circumstances of the good lookout at Caister station and if possible grant a little extra remuneration".

In 1883 the 'Covent Garden', on the No. 2 station, was replaced with a similar boat, again the gift of the Covent Garden Lifeboat Fund, and named 'Covent Garden'. In 1899 the same fund again replaced the boat, this time with a slightly smaller boat, built by Thames Ironworks for £1295.

A gift from Sir Reginald Proctor-Beauchamp, of Langley Hall near Norwich, resulted in the purchase of a boat to bear his name, 'Beauchamp', in 1892. This 36 foot boat was built by Critten for £266 and was, like all the previous boats stationed at Caister, of the Norfolk and Suffolk design. This new boat replaced the 'God Send'.

"4th November 1888...night very dark - launched with great difficulty. Sea sweeping right over boat. Cox asked crew if they should cross the Barber, crew consented, so they lashed themselves in the boat and sailed right through broken water shipping heavy sea all the time, drenched crew to skin..."

Sometimes the beachmen launched their boats only to find the boat they were seeking to assist had disappeared, probably managing to get itself off the sands. On many occasions the boats were at sea for long periods, as happened in 1888. At 6.30a.m. on Tuesday July 10th the yawl was launched to assist the steamer 'Lady Ann', 608 tons, on the Middle Cross Sand and they were engaged by the captain to try and get the ship off. At 5.00p.m. the lifeboat 'Covent Garden' reached the scene, looking for the yawl, and was asked to remain standing by until the ship came off the sands, which was achieved at 8.00a.m. on Thursday. The lifeboat returned to its station at noon, the beachmen having been at sea for a total of 53 hours.

On February 9th 1894, a Friday, at 11.30a.m. a steamer was reported on the north part of the Barber Sands. The beachmen launched their yawl and the lifeboat 'Beauchamp' at noon and were engaged to remain by the vessel for the remainder of Friday and all day Saturday, returning to station at noon on Sunday after taking 35 persons off the steamer and transferring them to a tug. The second lifeboat 'Covent Garden' was launched at noon on the Saturday to take 67 people off the steamer as the ship parted amidships, returning to station at 6.20p.m. Sunday. A busy weekend for the beachmen.

COMMUNICATIONS

The 1980s have seen revolutionary changes in all forms of communications, both on land and at sea, but a century ago things were very different. Telephone and radio links were unknown and visual and audible signals were necessary to communicate between the shore and ships at sea. The beachmen on watch during bad weather, especially at night or during fog, relied on hearing the guns and rockets fired from the lightships to signal a vessel in distress.

During foggy weather the light vessels fired warning guns at 10 or 15 minute intervals and the firing of a special rocket, of little sound but of great brilliance, immediately after a gun denoted that assistance from the shore was required. Guns were also fired when a vessel was seem to be standing into danger and the firing continued while two signal flags, S.D., of the then Commercial Code, "You are standing into danger" were hoisted.

Earlier fog signals used by the light vessels were bells, struck by hammers every half minute, and Chinese gongs about two feet in diameter sounded at short intervals. Over lesser distances these were very serviceable but the sound soon dissipated and had no range. Sirens, steam and compressed air whistles and gas guns were also used to try and warn shipping of imminent dangers.

It was to these audible signals that the beachmen responded although in some cases confusion meant long periods at sea with no results, as was the case on 21st March 1890.

The lifeboat 'Charles Burton', at Caister 1929-1941, was the last sailing lifeboat on the east coast.

"God Send launched after watch heard guns, although they did not know where from. A tug was called from Yarmouth and towed the lifeboat to the Wold lightship at midnight - they had not heard anything. Went to Cockle who had heard guns but did not know where from so towed to the Newarp. While talking to them heard guns to the north so went back to the Wold. Found a steamer on N.Hasbro Sand with the Winterton and Palling boats with her. Returned to station. Launched 9.30p.m. Friday, returned 9.30p.m. Saturday."

Communication on shore was somewhat worse with many messages being sent by hand, causing delays of many hours before the beachmen could respond to a vessel in need.

"February 1879 - sent two men to Yarmouth with horse and cart for a tug."

"March 25th 1879 - a man came to Caister station from Winterton and reported a vessel lying dismasted inside the Hasbro Sand."

"January 16th 1881 - ...letter received by messenger from Palling saying that there were two ships on the Hasbro Sand that no one had been to." (In this instance the 'Godsend' was launched at 4a.m. and returned 16 hours later having saved 21 lives.)

Wireless telegraphy was first used as a means of calling for the assistance of a lifeboat in 1899 when the East Goodwin lightship was fitted with transmitting equipment. Towards the end of 1900 the Marconi Wireless Telegraph Co. Ltd. established seven coastal stations along the British coastline, intended to experiment with ship to shore communication.

One of these stations was at Caister, in a house named Pretoria Villa, in the High Street. The main aerial mast was 150 feet high, the aerial suspended between this and a shorter mast to the east. The front room of the house contained the main apparatus and was also used as the operating room; the engine for charging the accumulators was situated in an adjoining shed, the accumulators themselves being in a specially constructed annexe. The remainder of the house was used as a dwelling for the officer in charge. The range of communication was 150 to 200 miles on the long wave (600M) and 100 miles short wave (300M).

In 1906 the Cross Sand lightship (15 nautical miles from Caister) was equipped with telegraph apparatus and was able to communicate with the Caister station. One of the first recorded instances where the Caister beachmen used wireless telegraphy was in 1909.

"At 3.30a.m. the second cox observed steamboat ashore on Cross Sand and near lightship. Called coastguard to communicate with the Marconi Station here but they could get no reply from Cross Sand. Launched yawl and followed with lifeboat..."

On this occasion two steamers had been in collision and the lifeboat was able to offer assistance. In January the following year, at 9.15a.m., the Marconi operator informed the lifeboat coxswain that a vessel was ashore on the Cross Sand. This was the S.S. 'Orkla' of Leith, loaded with coal.

Caister Rocket Brigade, March, 1933. *From left, standing:* A. Thompson, F. Humphrey, E. Julier, R. Bessey, A. Myhill, R. Trett, B. Nickerson, T. Smith, A. Dyball. *Seated:* R. Brown, C. Larkman, R. Chapman, J. Julier, Lieut. J. Maguire, MBE, RN, Station Officer T. Rowe, T. Jones, T. Humphrey, W. Horth, H. Bird.

In 1908 the radio station, as it had become known, was operated by Marconi International Marine Communication Co.Ltd. and Albert Searle was officer in charge. The following year the Post Office took over all coastal telegraph stations, including Caister. Telegraph equipment was removed from the Cross Sand lightship in 1915 and the Caister station changed to "general working" and was not used for ship to shore work. By 1920 wireless telephony had replace telegraphy and the Caister station closed some nine years later. Pretoria Villa had been connected to the Coastguard by a private Marconi telegraph wire during its early years but soon after the National Telephone Co. opened the first telephone exchange in the village in 1908 this was replaced with a telephone.

BEACH COMPANY DISASTERS

It has already been described how three founder members of the company were drowned in a yawl accident in 1847. Other such disasters were to befall the beachmen, one of which happened in July 1885.

On a calm summer night, July 21st, a schooner was seen to be aground on the Barber Sands. The beachmen sounded their call-out bell and the yawl 'Zephyr II' (purchased by the company in 1874) was launched with a crew of 15. On the way to the stranded vessel they had to pass close to the wreck of a schooner from which they had saved the crew some nine years previously, now only a stump of the mast showing above the water. Although they were all well aware of the position of the wreck and were

James Haylett of Caister. At the inquest following the loss of the 'Beauchamp', the suggestion was put to him that the lifeboatmen could have given up their mission and have been returning to the beach. His reply, variously quoted since, was to the effect that "Caister men never turn back!"

reminded by James Haylett to "keep a lookout for the sunken stump", for some unexplained reason the yawl struck the obstruction and almost immediately the boat filled with water and started to sink. The 15 men were thrown into the sea and one, John George, started to swim for the shore, the others desperately clinging onto anything they could find. John soon came across a Yarmouth shrimper and after being hauled aboard explained the situation to the two fishermen, who cut away their nets and sailed to the rescue of the stricken beachmen.

Six men were picked from the water but although the shrimper searched the area for some time no more survivors could be found. The beach company had lost eight men and the tragedy left six widows and 29 fatherless children in the village. An inquest was held the following day at the Kings Arms public house but despite evidence given by all the survivors there was no logical explanation for how the yawl had come to strike the old wreck on a calm summer night and a verdict of accidental drowning was reached. The centenary of the disaster was marked in 1985 when the chairman of the Volunteer Rescue Service laid a wreath at sea, accompanied by relatives of those who lost their lives.

Sixteen years later the company was to suffer another serious loss, this time involving the lifeboat 'Beauchamp'.

November 13th, 1901 was a dark winter's night and the Caister watch

The 'Beauchamp' served at Caister from 1892 until the tragedy of 1901.

saw rockets fired from the Cockle lightship and flares burning on a vessel stranded on the Barber Sands. The alarm bell was rung and the company was soon assembled on the beach to launch the lifeboat, an operation that because of the heavy seas took about three hours. Finally, after being washed back onto the beach many times, the boat was through the breakers and on her way to the Barber Sands, or so the shore crew thought, the darkness of the night having swallowed up all signs of the boat. Some 45 minutes later cries for help were heard from the shoreline and Frederick Haylett, together with his grandfather James Haylett, ran to a point only 50 yards north of where they had helped launch the lifeboat. There, in the surf, was the 'Beauchamp' bottom up and despite the heavy seas the two men dashed into the water. They were able to rescue three of the crew, Charles Knights, John Hubbard and Walter Haylett who, after being examined by the local doctor, Dr. H.W. Case, were sent home. The remaining nine crew members could not be seen.

Efforts to right the boat failed and this could not be accomplished until low water, several hours later. During this period five bodies were washed out of the boat onto the beach. The following morning ropes were fixed to the hull and the large crowd of villagers who had gathered on the beach hauled the lifeboat to an even keel. Three more bodies were found among the coils of rope in the boat; that of crew member Charles George was missing, having been washed out to sea.

The District Inspector of the R.N.L.I., Commander Holmes R.N., arrived in the village the next day and the County Coroner opened an inquest at the Lord Nelson public house in Beach Road. It was during this inquest that James Haylett, in answer to the suggestion that the boat might have been returning to the beach, is reputed to have used the words "Caister men never turn back", a phrase that has been synonymous with the spirit of the village lifeboatmen ever since. It was estimated that between 16,000 and 20,000 people were present at the funeral of the nine beachmen and a public appeal raised almost £12,000 for the widows and 44 fatherless children.

A short time later a Board of Trade enquiry was held at the Town Hall, Great Yarmouth, when every detail of the incident was examined and no blame could be directed on the boat, the crew or the R.N.L.I.

For his part in the rescue of the three survivors of the accident James Haylett was awarded the R.N.L.I. Gold Medal, which he received from King Edward VII at a ceremony at Sandringham House in January 1902. Frederick Haylett was awarded the R.N.L.I. Live Saving Diploma and the same year a large memorial, carved in Italian marble, was erected in the north-west corner of the village cemetery. The east window of the parish church was renewed in 1903 and was dedicated to the disaster.

The vessel the lifeboat had been launched to assist on that wild

November night was thought to have been a Lowestoft smack, which managed to lay an anchor in deep water where she remained until daylight and was then seen to sail away, apparently unaware of the drama that had occured on the beach only a few hours previously.

The 'Beauchamp' had been to the aid of 81 vessels and saved 146 lives during the nine years it was stationed at Caister but following the accident it was withdrawn from lifeboat service and for many years following was used as a pleasure craft on the Norfolk Broads. In 1961 the owner offered the boat to the proposed Maritime Museum for East Anglia and it was stored for several years at the rear of Gorleston library awaiting restoration, but eventually the deterioration of the hull and the strong views held about preservation by the Caister beachmen led to the remains being broken up.

THE TWENTIETH CENTURY

The Caister beachmen moved into the early years of the 20th century with the disaster of the 'Beauchamp' as a very real reminder of the dangers of their occupation. The volume of salvage work had dramatically declined from its peak in the mid 1800s and many East Anglian beach companies had disbanded, those remaining finding the majority of their work was now concerned with lifesaving, in conjunction with the R.N.L.I. lifeboats.

In 1903 a replacement lifeboat for the 'Beauchamp' was brought to the village. This was named 'Nancy Lucy' and presented by Sir Henry W.Lucy J.P. of London, being built by Thames Ironworks for £1603. It was of the Norfolk and Suffolk design, a style of lifeboat favoured by the Caister beachmen in preference to the self-righting types, despite the disaster of 1901.

The value of beach company shares had fallen sharply from their 19th century level when, as stated earlier, a single share had been sold for £84. In 1877 a share was sold by Samuel George's widow Sarah to William Wilson for £75, but by 1905 when William's widow Charlotte sold the same share to George Green it was only worth £20. (William Wilson had been drowned in the 'Beauchamp').

As the salvage work of the companies declined so did the need for any specialised boats other than lifeboats. The yawls that had served the beach companies so well for many years began to disappear rapidly from the East Anglian coastline, those that remained being converted for summer pleasure tripping or turned into houseboats on the Broads.

At Caister the yawl 'Glance' was sold in 1902 and so, in 1916, was the 'Wasp', a general purpose boat that had once been used for landing fish on Yarmouth beach before being obtained by the beach company. This left the company with only their yawl 'Eclat', a gig 'Ubique' and two lifeboats. In 1927 the 'Eclat', which the company had owned since 1886, one of the last yawls in salvage service, was sold and two years later the 'Ubique', damaged beyond repair during a launch, was sold for scrap wood.

Salvage work had almost come to an end, the R.N.L.I. ruling that its lifeboats were not to be used for salvage work except when no other aid was available. In exceptional circumstances when they were used for this kind of work a payment had to be made to the Institution to cover any damage or risk incurred. The crews themselves could make salvage claims if appropriate, but this only happened occasionally, one reason being that by making such claims they forfeited any payment they would otherwise have received from the R.N.L.I. for that service and they were held responsible for any damage to

The lifeboat 'Nancy Lucy' being winched up to the wooden slipway beside the 'white shed'. The latter was in use as a base for the lifeboatmen from 1887 until 1940.

the boat and, when motor lifeboats were introduced, for any fuel used.

Sometimes, after struggling to launch their boats for many hours, the weather forced the beachmen to give up. On these rare occasions the message "Caister failed to launched" was recorded in the log. The opposite was recorded on December 10th, 1910. "... launched in exceptionally quick time - inside 15 minutes."

The 1914-18 war saw the lifeboats launched many times to assist minesweepers and naval patrol boats in difficulty on the sand banks. "1917 March 16th - Submarine F3 on the Barber".

In 1919 the 'Covent Garden' was withdrawn and replaced by the 'James Leath', a boat transferred from the Pakefield station. This was again of the Norfolk and Suffolk design, having been built in 1910 and paid for by a legacy of James Leath, a Londoner. The boat weighed eight tons and required a crew of 13. This proved to be the last boat on the No.1 station, which was closed by the R.N.L.I. in 1929, leaving the beachmen with one lifeboat after 62 years of having two at Caister. The 'James Leath' later worked from the Aldeburgh station and in 1983 was put on permanent display at the National Lifeboat Museum in Bristol.

When the No.1 station was closed the remaining boat, 'Nancy Lucy', was replaced by the 'Charles Burton', a 38 foot boat of the Liverpool design, built in 1904 and transferred from Grimsby to Caister. This was to be the last sailing and rowing lifeboat in East Anglia.

In 1935 the company was given notice to vacate their lookout and store shed by the Lord of the Manor, Anthony Traynier. This building, that had stood on the beach for almost a century, was originally erected under verbal agreement with the Lord of the Manor and no written document was in existence defining the rights of the beach company. In lieu of rent the lord had been entitled to a one-fortieth share of all money earned by the company, but with the decline in salvage work this had become a very small annual payment. Mr. Traynier had purchased the manorial rights some years earlier and was anxious to improve the beach and make it more attractive to visitors.

At first the beachmen refused to give up possession of the headquarters but were then summonsed to appear in the County Court in May of that year. It was stated in court that as the beach company was not a legal entity and not an incorporated company, it was really an illegal association, therefore the possesion order would have to be made against a representative four members of the company, Charles Hodds, Charles Laycock, Charles Haylett and Joseph Woodhouse.

After much discussion the beachmen realised they could not win the case brought against them and a settlement was made by consent. The building was soon removed from the beach and the company then asked the R.N.L.I. for permission to use the lifeboat shed as a headquarters. This was agreed and the call-out bell, given to the company in 1883, was erected at the rear of the lifeboat shed. This building, known locally as the white shed, had been erected in 1887 to replace an earlier mid-19th century brick building owned by the Norfolk Shipwreck Association which collapsed in 1917 and was situated near the Gap. The "white shed", a timber building, served the company and the R.N.L.I. until 1940 when it was replaced, almost on the same site, by the lifeboat shed that stands on the beach today. The earlier buildings were only used to store the gear, the lifeboats themselves standing on the beach.

The Caister company was now the sole survivor of the numerous East

Anglian beach companies. Times were changing and a war loomed ahead, in many places motor lifeboats were replacing the old sailing types, bringing with them a great reduction in the manpower required to crew and launch them. The sailing and rowing boats needed a crew of 17 and a launching team of up to 23 men whereas the motor lifeboats only required a crew of eight and a launching team of 12, which included the tractor driver.

The war resulted in a shortage of local men and on many occasions soldiers billeted in the village helped to launch the lifeboat and even

The ropes, masts and oars of the lifeboat 'Charles Burton'. She was stationed at Grimsby prior to Caister.

supplemented the crew. The 'Charles Burton' was withdrawn in 1941 and replaced with the motor lifeboat 'Jose Neville'. This new boat, of the Liverpool type, was built with the aid of a legacy of Mrs. Ellen Neville of Barnes, Surrey, and brought a major change to the Caister station. For the first time the launching crew did not have to manhandle the boat across the beach and into the water; a tractor pushed the boat, mounted on a special trailer, into the water, saving considerable time and energy.

The beachmen realised the old beach company days were over and a

Above: Members of the lifeboat crew in 1906, wearing their medals for the rescue of the crew of the brig 'Annaprecht'. *From left, front:* 'Spratt' Haylett (Cox'n), James Haylett, Walter Haylett. *Back:* J. Plumber, A. Clews (Hon.Sec.), Soloman Brown. *Below:* Caister Lifeboat Coxswains 1919-1969. *From left:* Jack Plumber, 1956-1969, Jimmy Brown, 1950-1956, Joe Woodhouse, 1935-1949, Charles Laycock, 1919-1935.

The 'Jose Neville', a Liverpool class lifeboat stationed at Caister from 1941 to 1964. The last of this class has now been withdrawn by the RNLI, so Caister's 'Shirley Jean Adye' is the sole lifeboat of this type operational in the U.K.

decision was made to disband the company. Their last assembly as a company had been in 1940 when they were alerted for a Spitfire from R.A.F. Coltishall that had ditched in the sea off Horsey. Before the boat could be launched news was received that the plane was ashore and their services were not required. The R.N.L.I. call-out money was doled out in accordance with the rules, the last time money was to be shared out in this way. After almost 150 years the company was no more. The lifeboat however still had to be crewed and the war years were a busy time for all lifeboat stations, many launches being to rescue baled out air crew as well as ships in trouble. When a Thunderbolt fighter pilot baled out near Scratby a Supermarine Walrus amphibian was sent to rescue him, unfortunately could not cope with the rough seas and was itself washed ashore. The Caister boat was called to tow the Walrus to deep water while the fighter pilot was picked up by a boat launched from Scratby beach.

In 1964 the 'Royal Thames', a motor lifeboat of the Oakley design, replaced the 'Jose Neville'. This new boat was a gift from a Mr.Jackson of Hampshire, Miss Ellison of Sussex and a legacy of Mr.Forster of Kent. The R.N.L.I. only kept the 'Royal Thames' at Caister for five years. On October 17th 1969, despite fierce local opposition, the boat was withdrawn and the Caister station closed as it was considered the Gorleston lifeboat could adequately deal with the area. The 1960s had seen many changes in lifeboat organisation, new stations opened, many equipped with fast inshore rescue

Above: The service on 28th July 1957 for the centenary of the RNLI Caister Station. The lifeboat is the 'Jose Neville'. *Below:* The 'Royal Thames', the last RNLI lifeboat at Caister, on station 1964-1969.

A combined operation for Caister boat day, with the Gorleston RNLI lifeboat 'Barham' exercising with Caister's 'Shirley Jean Adye'. (Poppyland Photos)

boats, and 11, including Caister, closed.

Local beachmen had argued their case for keeping the lifeboat on the fact that the 'Royal Thames' was especially suited to work in the shallow waters around the sandbanks whereas the Gorleston boat was more suitable for deeper water. The inshore fishermen supported the beachmen and a petition was sent to the Queen, but to no avail.

The rescue of three men from an inshore fishing vessel in August 1969 brought to 1,815 the number of lives saved by the Caister station from 1858, a record for any lifeboat station in the British Isles. The last R.N.L.I. coxswain was Jack Plumber who had held the position from 1956, being awarded the R.N.L.I. Bronze Medal in 1963 and the B.E.M. in the 1969 birthday honours.

A public meeting was called in the village and a committee of ten men appointed to look into the possibility of operating a volunteer lifeboat to fill the gap left by the R.N.L.I. The boat house, owned by Great Yarmouth Borough Council, was offered to the beachmen at a peppercorn rent and the R.N.L.I. left the caterpillar tracked carriage, a set of oilskins and several other items of useful equipment. All that was required was a boat.

As soon as the lifeboat had left the station a 16 foot fibreglass dinghy owned by "Skipper" Woodhouse took its place, to maintain the tradition of running a lifesaving service from Caister, albeit of a limited nature. Both the actions of removing the R.N.L.I. lifeboat and the formation of a volunteer service were not, and probably never will be, unanimous village decisions. There will always be those who argue that it is not necessary for a lifeboat at Caister in these days when fast inshore and deep water boats are stationed close by.

A national appeal was launched to raise £50,000 to build a new lifeboat for the volunteer service but this was unsuccessful. Children from Caister High School raised enough money to purchase an inflatable inshore rescue boat, which during the summers of 1970 and 1971 saved four lives, and the fibreglass dinghy proved its worth in 1971 with four service launches.

In 1973 the Caister Volunteer Rescue Service, as the new company was known, purchased a 35 foot Liverpool type lifeboat that had been in service with the R.N.L.I. from 1953 to 1964 at St. Abbs in Scotland. This boat was renamed and formally launched on August 5th 1973 as the 'Shirley Jean Adye'. Re-engined, refurbished and repainted it once again established Caister as a lifesaving station. The members of the new Volunteer Rescue Service, although now a limited company and with twentieth century resources behind them, have many similarities with their predecessors, the beach company of the 18th and 19th centuries.

COASTGUARD AND ROCKET COMPANIES

Two organisations, not directly connected with the beachmen, but closely associated with their activities were the Coastguards and the Board of Trade Rocket Company, both of which were present in the village at the turn of the century.

The local coastguards, known in the early part of the last century as the Preventive Men, when their chief responsibility was to prevent smuggling and similar activities along the coastline, had in 1850 their own boat,

Today Caister has no rocket brigade of its own, but the Coastguard continue to provide this facility.
(Poppyland Photos)

warehouse and watch house on Caister beach, to the north of the Gap. When they were first established in the village is not recorded but the 1850s buildings were replacements for an earlier boathouse situated further eastwards and washed away by the sea. From at least 1836 there were six men and an officer stationed at Caister, coming under the jurisdiction of the Admiralty, and in 1881 a terrace of houses was built close to the beach to house the men. In 1923 the Board of Trade took over responsibility and the Caister station was reduced to two men and an officer.

In 1933 the Caister coastguard station was closed and a new station opened on the Brittania Pier at Great Yarmouth. The station officer, T. Rowe, was moved to the new Yarmouth station. Four years later an auxiliary station was opened at Caister and the old lookout reused; in 1938 a new lookout was built on Pin Hill and manned throughout the war years full time, being reduced to part time until 1955 with "Chippy" Brown in charge.

The Rocket Company was established in the later part of the 19th century and was under the control of the Board of Trade. Fishermen and beachmen were not allowed to become members of the Rocket Company, a measure to ensure that when required for service its members would not be at sea or employed with the lifeboat.

The rocket lifesaving apparatus was kept in a cart and pulled by horses along the beach to the required position. If the horses were otherwise engaged man-power was used. The rocket company was of limited use in this area but nevertheless played an important role in the lifesaving facilities that were available when required. The last time the apparatus was used on a wreck was in 1919 when the 'Moorside' was wrecked on Caister beach; the coastguard called them to assist and the lifeboat crew helped the rocket company bring the crew ashore.

Their last call out was in 1929 for the barge 'Scotia' ashore on Yarmouth north beach. The horses were not available and the company pulled their cart along the road to Yarmouth but upon arrival found the Gorleston lifeboat had taken the crew off the stricken boat.

The Rocket Company was disbanded in 1933 when the coastguard station closed, the apparatus being taken to Yarmouth. The company then consisted of 17 men with station officer T. Rowe in charge and had amongst its members many well-known names in the village such as Tommy Jones the newsagent and Tom Humphrey the village blacksmith.

This then completes the story of the Caister beachmen and hopefully illustrates some of the difficulties and challenges they had to face over a 200 year period. Caister looks set to continue its tradition of lifesaving work, perhaps for a further 200 years, during which period the challenges will always be present.